AN AMERICAN SOUTH

AN AMERICAN SOUTH

POEMS BY SYBIL KEIN

Michigan State University Press
East Lansing

Copyright © 1996 by Sybil Kein

All Michigan State University Press Books are produced on paper which meets the requirements of American National Standard of Information Sciences—Permanence of paper for printed materials ANSI Z39.48-1984.

Michigan State University Press
East Lansing, Michigan 48823-5202

02 01 00 99 98 97 96   1 2 3 4 4 5 6 7 8 9

Library of Congress Cataloging-in-Publication Data

Kein, Sybil.
    An American South : poems / by Sybil Kein.
        p.   cm.—(Lotus poetry series)
    ISBN 0-87013-412-4
    1. Louisiana—History—Poetry. 2. Creoles—Louisiana—Fiction.
    I. Title. II Series.
PS3561.E3757A84   1996
811'.54—dc20

                                                                96-6361
                                                                   CIP

america   as much a problem in metaphysics as
it is a nation earthly entity an iota in our
galaxy   an organism that changes even as i
examine it   fact and fantasy never twice the
same   so many variables . . . .

Robert Hayden
from *American Journal*

For my children
Elizabeth, David and Susan
with love

CONTENTS

ACKNOWLEDGMENTS

Merci beaucoup to Michel Fabre and Marvin E. Ellis for their help with the French and Creole editing.

I am grateful to Gwendolyn Brooks, Naomi Long Madgett, and Dudley Randall for their encouragement. I owe a special debt to Naomi. Her courage and her dedication to the art of poetry is an inspiration and constant source of strength for me.

To Robert Hayden, whose magic lives in memory, *merci.*

I

THUNDER

"Such strange things storms do,— here purifying the
air, yonder treading down rich harvests, now replenishing
the streams, and now strewing shores with wrecks; here a
blessing, there a calamity."

— G. W. Cable

1724

As she told her beads,
as he knelt by her side,
as the priest toned the
blessing of the marriage
by Holy Mother Church,
as the bell sounded for
Jean-Baptiste Raphael and
Marie Gaspard from *l'église*
of Saint Louis, together,
and with every breath that
moved within them, they
swore that none of their
issue would ever become
slave to those branded pests*
and vermin who hustle on these
muddied *rues*, none ever to be
minion to wild-eyed schemers,
pirates, or whoremongers in
This king's colony;
that they would save, hew,
blossom, safeguard, cling,
sweat, shield, fight and
die to defend this vital
freedom.
Oh, hold this liberty
forever in memory, in song,
in love and courage.
Creoles.
Gens de couleur.
Libres.

---

* "pest flotillas" — ships which brought the scum of Paris
   and the provinces to the colony, 1717 to 1721.

3

Père Duveny Ruminates Among the Natchez

Fort Rosalie, 1728

Love is a mystery
I cannot reckon,
like haze over cypress
or skeletons wrapped in

winter sermons on Job.
As if cursed, I walk this
road again, hearing polybeat
prayers to The Sun God, grisly

rituals for which I continually
hold grief. They will not let old
gods die. Now I ache with echoes
of soft brown maidens whose

kindness I often take at will.
Such ghost-grave mornings find me
sleepless in this lavish
woodland of war.

Coincoin

FOR MARIE MOORE-BOYD

1786.
You were finally free;
and you bought your
children, grandchildren.
And you meant not only freedom,
but land, money.
Code Noir, the humbled Capuchin,
the widow Buard stole your man,
your French lover, your Metoyer.
What lesser gods sang you
scornful favor then?
What Red River secrets
have you made ghosts,
sown deep in indigo,
pepper grass, and Palm-of-Christi?
Why do I pick and gouge
frantically at your bones
along these Natchitoches
rigolets? Am I still looking
for my proud grandmother, sister
who is called Marie-Thérèse?
Or does my soul lie grieving
in this fevered mud?

Après le Bal du Cordon bleu

New Orleans, 1792

Did the sun come up
or go down?
I am breaking like a woman.

I wake as from a dream.

What can I do now
that you have rejected me?

What choice have I as woman . . .

For months I thought of
nothing but meeting you,
to hold you fiercely,
to feel that ardour.

to be raped as slave or free?

My vision of a woman; of
chestnut skin, raven curls,
Oh fire-dark eyes, I would have
given anything to own you.

Is not "mistress" well kept . . .

It was not to be.
I lived and died in that waltz.

death still?

Oh midnight glow within my arms,
favorite of the gods, was it
your mother's charms hexed you
to perfection?

Oh women of African beauty carved,

And when the waltz was over
I begged for another. But you
in your Creole lilt, refused me.

paled by seeds of Europe's loins,

Your mother from the velvet
dais smiled, but custom
assured my world had ended.

why did our fathers breed us thus . . .

6

Aurora Felix, though that room
was filled with quadroons rare,
I sought and lost a love that
kings may claim.

     to be ever marked as pleasing whores
In my stumblings round the world
I shall seek but this one moment:
when love, fear, hope and despair
all met in the flash of your eyes.

     to flesh the eternal savage
     lust of men?

L'Enfant perdue

La Nouvelle Orléans, 1801

Ma fille?
Mo 'ti bébé qui
j'aime plus que
le Ciel ?

What must be done,
as many before me
have contrived.
Can my soul suspend

its grief till I am
no more? A ransom
for my only daughter
that she may be spared

those spiteful crimes
against flesh born dark?
Her father on his deathbed
begged me free her of

this sordid legacy.
How he cursed the name
of my one link to that
slaver's sin. I own no

logic to dispel the laws
of men who deem us such
a world; except the price*
is paid and Père Antoine

---

* The custom of giving "donations" to the Catholic Church to have
birth and baptismal records changed to exclude slave ancestors.

assured there is no trace
save what gossip follows
me to my grave. I too must
be scratched away.

She will come tomorrow
for the news. My heart
is thick and throbs in
my head. But I must remain

aloof, attentive to my
sewing — this little blue
and white *maison* pictured
in solitude, a remembrance

of me. I will say, "Know
that your mother loves you
above all the desperate
designs of men, and she does

pledge, if you will it,
to never see you again in this
life." Oh, I surely will go mad,
It is too much.

Dieu sais, je ne peut
pas dormir, pas dormir.
Ma fille?

On Watching Zelime Being Sold

La Nouvelle Orléans, 1804

Monsieur Charpentier's words
Are blurred on my ears.
The market is a fury of silk
hats, rigid bonnets and purses
dangling greed and quick perversion.

Sharp, gruff voices mangle
the eager laughter which burst
from the crowd without shame.
A ragged urchin tugs my sleeve
to sell a *chaud calas.** Horses

pound muddied streets, neighing
curses at the harsh heat. I watch
as beast-men invade what only
lovers should know: quickly exposed
breast, a trembling opened mouth,

terse, desperately silent cries.
I am flushed, full. The price goes
up. Brass cuffs click on her wrists.
For a moment her eyes meet mine.
Dieu! How my heart shrivels in my

bosom! I tried to stay this block,
but fortune fell and all was lost.
Vils Américains! They bring unkindly
senses. We'll have no justice now.

---

* Creole rice cake

My head pounds from the stinging
heat as the next soiled flesh
are shuffled up. She cannot
hear, "Forgive me," over this
rabble swarm. And it is I
they quickly lead away.

Rêve érotique d'une quarteronne de M. Lafcadio Hearn

To desire?
Voir la lumière sous mo lapeau?
Caressér chaque pointe noir où le mouile
li ramassé comme yé gouttes de feu.

Avec to voix comme un vent murmurant
toi, mon amour, to trouvé
tout mo tristesse et
goûtée sur to langue les petits soupirs de mon
copuion, tout tremblant, mo bouche, mes z.yeux.

Mo est la lune chaud desous to doights-yé,
puis to ramassé-moin lentement et descendre
dedans mes bras-yé, mes jambres, mes cheveux.
Nous levér de notre d'l'eau dangereux
et cette nuit envelopper nous dans mollesse
des étôiles.

Lafcadio Hearn's Dream of a Quadroon
Mistress

Your wish?
To touch the light under my skin?
To kiss each nude darkness where
moisture gathers like drops of fire?

With your voice like a hungry wind
you, my handsome lover, you alone
find my sadness and swallow on your
tongue the little sighs of my
virginity, my mouth, my eyes.

I am the warm moon under your fingers,
then you gather me slowly and
descend inside my arms, my thighs, my
hair. We rise from our dangerous waters
and this night envelops us in the softness
of stars.

Sons of Freedom

FOR APMSR

1812, New Orleans

With an eagle in their caps,
once more they rushed with
fowling pieces and flint to
share in the peril and glory,
to perhaps be counted as men,
fellow citizens, held in equal
esteem.

"Aux arms, citoyens!"

"We are natives of this Province
and our dearest interests are
connected with its welfare."

"En avant, grenadiers!"

Under the white banner of the Bourbons,
under the red and yellow of Spain,
as allies under the Stars and Stripes:

"Ça qui mourir . . ."

Thrown to the front, their red and white
silk flag towering before the a-rat-a-
tat-tat of the drum, this battalion of
Men of Color, free, fought for that moment
of brotherhood felt in the heat of battle,
that freedom bursting in air, to crush
the threat of the English.

" . . . n'a pas ration !"

But what is this paradox? Dreams
of valor, of fame? Did they win

even the hollow victory of martyrs?
Or in this American South were the
distant rumblings of Dixieland muffled
by the victory shouts for Old Glory?

> *"Ça qui mouri,*
> *Tant pis pou Yé!"*

Siblings: The Mulatto Slave

New Orleans, 1827

Why she drive me so
this vile *maîtresse* who
is as brown as chicory?
She works me till raw
flesh is peeled from
hands and knees and
strained back makes one
leg drag when I walk.
If I complain she
takes delight in cursing
me as freak. I dare not
tell her that I think
her very color is evil;
that nose too — the devil's
thumb. Each morning we must
have coffee hot and strong
brought to bed and once a
week have fresh pralines
for our cousins from Amite.
If she but knew the little
bubbles at the center of
her morning cup that she
considers "luck" were first
coughed up by me; and added
to the crunch of those Sunday
candies are stiff short hairs
which one day will conjure ill.

I have not twenty years, yet see
my hands all chipped and burnt.
I've heard stories how these
gens de couleur libres have
bought slaves to set them free
but I have not encountered this.
My life is hard and peaceless
at her commands. But *"Bon Dieu Bon"*
and next time she reaches for the
Cat because I did not lower my
bastard eyes enough when she
spoke, I'll rip her lips apart.
Blunted hands may make good weapons,
and what is freedom but vengeance
sought and won; I'll pay the price.

Les Soeurs de la Sainte Famille

Before the Civil War,
Creole nuns with loyal waifs
stood on the streets
of the Old Quarter begging.
They wiped the spit
from their bonnets with "God-
bless-you's" to heathen
drunks and fare-you-well
ladies staggering in
the New Orleans summer sun.
Soeur Delille. Soeur Gaudin. Soeur Charles.
"Don't they know
'tis crime to tend nigger slaves
and natural half-breeds
whom we count as missing chattel?
Haughty *femmes de couleur
libres!* Would have them sold and
whipped should law permit;
or made fine whores for gentlemen-
of-means, *n'est pas?*
Damned infernal heat is why the vomit
comes. Here's for your
cup and cause, Madame." God bless
Aidez-nous, cher Bon Dieu Seigneur, aidez-nous.
Faith and love
they did prevail till now.

Zalli

She grows pale in that house
behind the palmettos. Age crawls
lightly on her skin; the silver brim
of hair glows against her face despite
the henna oils.

Jean is dead, and the gift of the house*
has kept her from the dance halls, from
begging. Her daughter taught
sustaining love in careful caring.
Life has not been shallow.

Memory lives in things once treasured:
an emerald broach, a lavender fan
encrusted in pearls, lace gloves incensed
from High Mass at the Cathedral's
baptisms, weddings, deaths.

Daily rituals of coffee, market, *soirées*,
now include visits to the apothecary's and
Madame Ruth's for herbs and fortune-telling.
Her hands shake violently after just one
anisette, and a dizziness comes on waking.

Sighs are deeper too; and pangs of
unclaimed love, family, the heart-hurts
grow louder, linger. Years are burdens
which press the shoulders, slow the legs.
Each task demands thought, afterthought.

---

* Madam John's Legacy — French Quarter, New Orleans.

19

Eyelids fold downward on eyes that are
not startled at the everyday crimes of
selfish men, and these eyes stare deeply,
like candle flames into the distant darkness,
balancing movement with fear.

II

LIGHTNING

"The sky grew dark. The lightning raced to the
seventeen quarters of the heavens and the lake heaved like
a mighty herd of cattle rolling in a pasture."

— Zora Neale Hurston

An American South

FOR JASON KERRY MOORE

Louisiana

Banana plantains, crepe myrtle
in pink bounty, palmettos
bracing clear sky, mornings
bright with mocking birds,
finch, cooing doves, laurel,
thick figs, pears, peach
flowers.

All this of a spring to cache
memory of chains, bloody hunks
of hair, flesh turned with earth
for planting sweet peas, bodies
of babes wrung limp and plowed
under, eyes, ears, hands rotting
in the sun, genius crushed by law.

In this land of cotton, church bells
clang a blusey jazz, while red-blooded
bougres-à-lea * take their stand, ready
to loose well harvested beasts of hate.
Thick dancing children give back hurt
with fists of fear and random death.
To live and die in Dixie?

---

* Swamp people

23

Witness, O Spring,
what men do as easy as living,
breathing, some with a laugh that
sears the wind and mocks the eternal
dignity of the soul.

Send pestilence, plague, storm.
No. Righteous anger only sleeps.
When aroused, mortals will war
upon these crimes until Earth's careful end.

Oh countless named and unnamed
humanity who by your deaths have
rendered pause, have you also
forgiven? Will this South ever,
ever be reconciled?

Toucoutou*

"Ah, Toucoutou, yé connain
vous, to té un morico!
Y'a pas savon qui t'assez
bon pou blanchi to lapeau!"
— Joseph Beaumont

Pale.   Pale beyond relief.
Eyes stretch into the mirror,
etch rose-bud mouth,
small French nose,
Indian-brown hair
curved to frame the portrait.

Cached   behind the face,
ghost-grey slave
ancestors cause sudden
puffs of color to cheeks;
blush the eyes
with bitter tears.

Must,   must look away.
taut blue veins
under faint skin
deny what truth
the court revealed;
dignify grim vanity.

---

* The nickname for the free-woman-of-color who was unaware of her
African blood, and brought suit to retain her status as white. Antebellum
New Orleans.

Image   narrows to vanishing
point. Anger is impotent
against violent hatreds:
chime, vaunt, proclaim
this infinite untouchable
privilege of being
white.

Swamp Legend

She was a tall
freckled woman; had
arms like a man.
Could catch a
water moccasin by
the throat; hold
it till it was dead.

Dead. She found
her son. Hanging,
neck broke; his
innocence erect and
stuffed into his
lipless mouth. She
peeled off his skin-clothes;
buried him in red mud.

Disappeared after that.
Let her hair
grow wild; ate
mice; crowed at
the moon; climbed
those thick oaks,
until her eyes
bled like fire.

Ti Malice

Trappé, comme un chien battu,
un vieux bougre à so lit,
li assis muet, placide, embarrassé.

So lapeau gris pâle, blessé
avec piques-yé du temps;
lasang-bleu glacé dans so mains.

Plié sou so maigre ventre,
z.os fragile sont plissé,
défiguré; so pieds rigides.

So z.yeux sombre, yé ouvri et fermé
lentement, paroles sans larmes.
Li trappé moin avec so douleur étrange.

C'est pas mon pére ici,
mais un mystère, un mauvais
coup d'esprits violents.

Méchants fantômes, yé espère
dans l'espace lourd entre nous.
Mo sorti avec silence dedans mes z.yeux.

Ti Malice*

Trapped like a beaten dog,
an old man on his bed
sits mute, calm, embarrassed.

His ashen skin is wounded
with the stings of time;
blue blood frozen in his hands.

Bent under his thin stomach,
his fragile legs are folded,
twisted; his feet stiff.

His deep eyes open and close
slowly, words without tears.
He traps me with his strange pain.

This is not my father here,
but a mystery — an evil trick
of violent spirits.

Those spiteful ghosts are waiting
in the heavy space between us.
I leave with silence inside my eyes.

---

* A spiteful spirit, hero of some of the folktales of Haiti and Louisiana.

29

Mala

Port Hudson, 1809

Oh, she's a strange lot.
Still mutters "cuartada"*
and some other Spanish
nonsense. Josh was a
fool to buy this one.
Hard enough for us folk
to get used to "silver
plays" and "mercys," never mind
the jigger-dangles of cargo
from the Cuban trade.
Whipped her good I did on
yesterday. Refused to work
again; begged to tend her
children. Well, what children?
I was to market when the little
suckers were sold; not to us,
mind you. Could tell trouble
then; threw down next to Josh's
boot with such a wailing and
braying. He kicked her soundly
so she'd hurt to yelp about.
Look at her now, mumbling and
swaying, grunting at the oak.
Calling black devils, no doubt.
I declare, there's more'n evil
in her. Josh would kill her

---

* Under Spanish law in Cuba, a slave was allowed to pay each month a
  small amount of the price originally paid for him or her and thus buy
  freedom.

but my Christian reason often
stays his hand. I even sent
a buck to jump and breed, but
nothing came of it. Some more
trusted ones tell us how she
crouches down nights with piglets,
cuddles them, coos some la la
ditties in their dirty ears, puts
them on her teats — its shameful.

Such a godsend you are to take
her off my hands. My feelings
sometimes unfit me for a slave-
holder. There's a plague in it . . .
Come fetch the wench tomorrow. The
sun is waxing orange in the east.
Best to wait this rattling of the dust.
'Tis sudden storm.

". . . Plantation home, cabins, all were mere
standing ash. A surging tide of fire and
winds had pitched like hell. None was left
save one depraved negress. She was found
naked, and making savage gyrations in the
sty amid the pink and lifeless corpses
strewn within."

Les Vagabonds

Etienne:
Sailing to France, *enfin,*
to Paris *encore.* No more
made to beg, made to step
aside; the freedom of five
generations is empty in this
south. Now this hated pass,
paper to nick and sunder man-
hood. Criminals! Your slaves
outnumber you and will become
clawing beasts upon your backs.
Rather a pauper in a free land
than remain where hate is as hot
as this August heat! *Assez!*

Aristide:
Something we must do to strike
down this latest vicious law.
Surely reason must prevail?
Are we not loyal sons? Human
curtsey, Sirs, take only those
who have offended, not all free
and useful citizens. Are we not
in this alike?

Eugénie:
Pass? Oh no. I will not
carry a pass. Don't they
know I am free? And I too
have slaves? Let them
haul me to the calaboose.

My true grandfather is
government judge. Tear that silly thing into
pieces. I will not touch it.

Isidore:
What will be next?
Badges on our arms
to show whiteness, blackness?
Are we not Americans?
If one drop of black blood
makes us slaves, will one
drop of white blood make us
free? I own no slaves nor have
I harmed any man.
What is this whiteness? A weapon
of evil? A cold disguise of God?
The pelt of fear?

33

A Portrait of Madam Boucard, with Pearls

We are alone.
1890. A new year.
Emile is here
one hour before midnight
with last year's censure.
I am numb, unmoved.
He wants me to be his
masterpiece, pure wife,
passionate mistress.
I am not her. I cannot be
paragon. I will never forget
his violence nor trust his
belated conversion. Will he
pervert my tenderness again?

He sips his champagne to toast
this new decade. I decline.
I read Voltaire as he stares
and rants. Dry anger sits on
my eyelids like age upon stone.
He dare not touch me.

Madam Boucard's Assignation

1892

I stand in my rose
garden admiring new
buds. Emile is amazed
at how each week that
he is away I plant one
more Joy-of-Morning or
Beauty's Flame.

He does not know these
are in memory of each
night I stole with my
dark lover. In a year,
a thousand roses shall
bloom here. For his

sins I will bed the Cross
of Christ upside down amid
the oleander. Should there be
azaleas for each mistress?
Mirabilis for his bastard babes?

Madam Boucard to
Her Mulatto Daughter

1909

Some unnamed thing,
some word or deed
needled in memory
too painful to learn.
Is this silence
mine or yours?

Was childhood's only sweets
those cruel laws which
distanced you from me?
Was it I who menaced you
to mute what dreams give?

Do you see me now,
horrid ringmistress,
numb trickster who
danced to your wide-
eyed pain? A weak monster
then, who drowned in fear
and could not save herself
or you?

Tell me what chants to sing,
what prayers to carve in stone
to heal us both?

I have mothered as best
I could, giving what I
guessed were pretties
and ease. Give me then,
a voice in words or deeds
to kill this unnatural
coldness. Make us love.

36

III

HEAT

"The sun shines, I raise again my head;
For next to evil, God has placed good."

— B. Valcour

View From the Ramparts

New Orleans, 1818

Carmelita Peña
quarteronne and mistress,[1]
sat in solitude in her
pink bricked patio, drinking
flaxseed tea.

The child she was bearing
would be a son this time,
she carried high and heavy.
And Madam Marie had swung
the egg three times low.

Such torment the first had
been, day sickness, vapors,
pains. This one was calmer,
kicked less. She craved for
lemons and starch.

John would not make demands
as often, would not destroy
his seed which was only with
her; the first, a daughter;
this one, namesake, legal heir.

Confinement pleased her,
though she also carried
stings of malicious conte[2]
from outside these walls.

---

[1] Mistress of John McDonogh
[2] gossip

39

They would destroy her if
she were less secure.

But she wore what female
dignity she had as glove
against such hate. She was
no less woman from the rest,
no less lover, no less friend.

And she was free. Her children
would not sop the slim crust
of slavery, but dine on crêpes
and sip Madeira, call for servants
to scatter about and please.

And they would read. They
would read and write and
learn the alchemy of wealth,
choose kindness over curses,
and go abroad, unbound.

At Rowan Oak

FOR THADIOUS M. DAVIS

Within earshot below,
window to window,
the plank cabin sits watchdog
behind the Faulkner house.
Time was, the lilac wallpaper
was neatly in place and the
slick green linoleum squared
the floors. And she rocked by
the fireplace, and burned
a fire that spit chunks of
sparks and huffed black smoke
over those great magnolia trees.

"Why the hell is Mammy Cally
burning a fire hot as it is tonight?"
Miss Estelle is a stone at the bedroom
window, does not answer him.

They do not see the face, unmasked
in her freedom from them; do not know
how she grips the arms of that chair
until her wrists shake;
how the sweat steams through her apron
to form little rainbows with the drops
from her brow, her eyes; how she
becomes the fire to send her true soul
floating away from the farm, from Oxford,
from Mississippi, from the south.

The stilted love she feels for them is etched
on her body's thick shell; words sugar
from her lips and they, the world, feel
safe, less unlucky. In the meantime, she
drawls and stomps, rocks and burns as the
twin possums of hate and love gorge and
emerge from that sweet bosom of the night.

Spells

CHANT:
Chicory root, guinea pepper,
crossing oil, filé;
Holy water, Big John root,
rooster's blood, bay leaves.
Sacred Heart, Saint Expédite,
Legba, Ézili;
Please grant my favor,
âgo, 'si soit-il.

I.
Alcide raped Ursulé's girl,
five years old. Nobody believed
the child except Hélène.
She wrote his name nine times on
cigarette paper and stuffed it
in a lemon, walked those wooden
planks at the Dumaine Street warf
and threw the lemon into the river.
She put him in the mouth
of a dead black hen and let it rot
in the sun. Under moonlight,
she burned a black candle
on his portrait and buried it
upside down. In three days, he
wandered dark streets with his
mouth open. Words stretched to rusty
sounds in his throat; and all
of his hanging parts festered,
shrivelled, and turned to dust.

43

II.

Her husband's whore passed
a sickness on to Lilan which made her
barren. Père Junise told her
to forgive him, but other gods thought
otherwise. She boiled his shoes
in cayenne pepper and flaxseed, made a
salt cross on his pillow, tied
his pubic hair in a white handkerchief
and burned it in a cabbage leaf.
She put a menage of Congo root and Indian
turnip on the doorsteps of the woman.
In the middle of the night, nine days
later, Pierre bent over his crazed
mistress as she carved a bloody half moon
on his throat.

III.

Her fat brown skin
was peeling away from bones
in patches, like a snake;
was covered with white powder
and lard. Paulette had no sleep in
eight days. Herbs did no good;
nor did the priest-doctor.
She could only talk in hoarse hisses;
didn't need to make it plain.
In her scaley hands, the Mulatto Queen
put a small red bag. *Gris-gris.*
On the ninth day, Madam Selina
who lived across Bayou Road,
red tongue darting out of her mouth,
coiled up in her bed and died.

CHANT:
Chicory root, guinea pepper,
  crossing oil, filé;
Holy water, Big John root,
  rooster's blood, bay leaves.
Sacred Heart, Saint Expédite,
Legba, Ézili;
Please grant my favor,
  âgo, 'si soit-il.

45

Bayou Ballad

Oh, have you heard,
and it was not long ago,
how they killed the sweetest singer
of Cajun zydeco?

Amédée Ardoin was brought to play
a *fais-do-do* near Mamou. The summer's
heat bore through the roof and walls
of that wooden-tin dance hall.
The waltzers and two-steppers did
not notice through their whiskey eyes
that the singer who had not moved
from his seat before the crowd was
soaked to the skin in sweat, was blinded
by the salty water beading on his face.

By and by, one dark *joli blon* did glance
at this and of habit to others carelessly
offered a white handkerchief to him as he
smiled between songs.
The *fête* went on with the gaiety of hees
and haws, claps and howls as he chuned
and soothed many a weary soul.

But then, when it was over, when the moon
shone high through the still, piney
woods, rough white hands found his neck,
fists of hate punched his head, his
groin, his chest, pearlized boots kicked
his breathless body on the ground. He
played dead, but not dead enough.
They drove the wheels of a late T-model
over his throat, back and forth to a
refrain of regular curses and "That'll
teach you never take no handkerchief
from no white woman, nigger!"

46

And so it was in this Luzianna, this
south. He lived long enough to tell
of it in ghost words, in signs. His
accordion stabbed and mangled,
died too.

The killers never suffered, never gave
it a second thought. Did not those back
roads see many a bloody night? Did not
God and country make the rules as plain
as skin and hair? Was it not fair to
defend our womanhood against this
deadly evil?

Is this a song that never ends?

Oh, have you, have you heard,
and it is not long ago,
how they killed the sweetest singer
of Cajun zydeco? Ahieeeeeeeeee!

Homage to Marie Laveau

Isis of the south,
carrying baskets of
hope, healing salts
from ancient waters,
salve for the evil
we do to ourselves:

À toi la gloire, et
la paix du Seigneur soit
toujours avec vous.

Mother of mysteries,
pouring comforting rain
to calm the terror of
the innocent betrayed:

À toi la gloire, et
la paix du Seigneur soit
toujours avec vous.

Marie, crowned in red
silk turban, golden hoops
from the sun, queen whose
words give power to the
powerless:

À toi la gloire, et
la paix du Seigneur soit
toujours avec vous.

Bearer of food to
the destitute, chance
to the luckless, aid
to those imprisoned,
Mother of Justice, Right,
Truth:

À toi la gloire, et
la paix du Seigneur soit
toujours avec vous.

Protector of the weak,
You whose tenderness un-
tangles the snares of Fate,
who lets loose the pleasant
winds of the seas to free
us from doubt and fear:

À toi la gloire, et
la paix du Seigneur soit
toujours avec vous.

Letter to Alice Ruth Moore

14 April, 1894

The grief of Spring's upon us as I write;
And yet more grief for what I hold most dear,
To see you clothed again in shadow's night
And thereby free my soul from ruinous fear.
Such joy is fragile, shy, wears memory well,
And bids us live on promises and pain.
But please, my dear, give thought to plainly tell
That you'll remember — sadly or in vain.
Here 'tis lovely, buds grow quietly sweet,
And purple lilacs swell the air at noon.
Fair apple blossoms faint beneath the heat,
And robins fly to nest on trees in bloom.
With this I send to you a heartfelt plea —
Be well and if you can, remember me.

From the French Market

FOR MARY LOUISE BAHAM LEWIS

Cinnamon ladies
in gingham bonnets
and white aprons
singing their *fleurs,*
calas or ginger cakes,
sitting on the banquettes
or walking under the eaves
of the Indian Market amid
Misu's, Herrmeisters, Chiefs,
and thieves, in their butter-soft
Créole language:
"Calas, Tout chaud!"
or in Spanish:
"Flores, Gardenias, Jasmines"
or in French:
"Petit gâteaux, Pralines,"

whatever the visitor should please.

These *marchandes* would save
picayunes enough to one day
buy a sister or a son or
herself. Did Madam know
that every praline bought
meant a sweeter step to
liberty for one so hated?
That even under sun-boiled heat,
through days of rain and mud,
heavy fevered air that caught them
short of breath and sick-weary,
they remained?

51

That they became fixed as
present day stuffed Mammy Dolls,
big as life and still the butt
of horrid jokes that belie what
dignity crowned that checkered
rag, that Créole kerchief, *tignon,*
mammy rag, nigger rag, dolls, play-
things, souvenirs?

Those earring hoops were made of
gold. Thick painted lips were
actually Senegalese small and
not rouged.
Bulging eyes were quite
proportioned, varied in color,
quick and clever.
And in that melodic speech
she was sure to answer your
vileness or evil and hurl curses
from old gods against you or
your progeny if you troubled her.

Oh, I would fear this caricature
despite her contorted face.
And do not mean her ill with back-
ward glance or words. Her anger,
now more than two centuries old
could send a plague, a killer storm,
or something unexplained and in the
very air.

IV

RAIN

"Dolo toujours courri larivière."
(Water always runs to the river.)
— Creole Proverb

Fiddler's Song: After a Flogging

Nothing in the moon
To calm me.
Other times I would
Spread moon hairs
Over me, little wisps
Curling on the edges
Of my chains.
I hardly know the moon
Now. A wailing tune
Sits dry in my mouth,
And little stars lie
Dead around my feet.

Wild Iris

Soft measured rain at dawn,
Sweet air floating on the wind:
Fragments of time filtering
Through these bayous.

Oh, what can my heart hear?

Madeline's salty song of life
Danced in Cajun calico dreams,
Innocence locked in legend
Where first love dies.

I was there meshed in moss,
Tricked by flowing moonlight,
Lush horizons, and thick male
Promises of peace.

Does memory flush and fold?

Oh, cruel country waltz
Of vengeance played insane.
Gifts of fetish and fowl
Cured no barren heart.

Some unseen thing, the savage ghost of pain?

Come sing me now,
Dark Madeline of the marsh.
Dim waters still the noise
Of fear remembered.

Songs of rain, songs of solace?

A seagull pauses
On a grassy stem
Whose indigo blossoms slowly
Break and fall.

Zelime

Zié à moin semble
fontainne, dipi
mo pli gardé to.
                    — Creole Folk Song

Were it not for your eyes,
Zelime,
Your green-grey eyes which
made little doors for me
to enter beyond my weary,
worrisome days,
I would have forgotten
the light that bonds us
one to another.

You reached for me despite
grave shadows of custom
and law. I would have sworn
against God and King to have
that light; but you preferred
our courtly meetings at Place
Congo, amid shouts and drums,
fires of fierce dance for our
stolen touches.
And then you were gone.

Each Sunday,
I linger at the Square,
grow old with thoughts of you,
Tire of the Bamboula,*
the rough Calinda.*

---

* Slave dances

Where are you now,
as the curfew booms?
Where are you now,
as my heart grows dark?

Chant d'une veille marchande

Parce que mo coeur est triste,
M'a vendre mes revenants:
Vingt-cinq cents pour les hommes,
Cinquante cents pour les femmes.

Tendez, comme y'apé prier,
Gardez, donc y'apé plaider.
Drôle, Monsieur, Madame,
Voulez-vous acheter?
Parce que mo coeur est triste,
M'a vendre mes revenants.

Pas mandé-moin qui yé té,
C'est ça mo dois oubliér.

Parce que mo coeur est triste,
M'a vendre mes revenants:
Vingt-cinq cents pour les hommes,
Cinquante cents pour les femmes.

Song of the Old Vendor

Because my heart is mournful,
I will sell my ghosts:
twenty-five cents for men,
fifty cents for women.

Listen, they're praying;
see how they beg.
Curious Master, Mistress,
will you buy?
Because my heart is grieving,
I must sell my ghosts.

Don't ask who they were;
that's what I must forget.

Because my heart is dying,
I will sell my ghosts:
twenty-five cents for men,
fifty cents for women.

Suzette

Ah, Suzette, chère
amie, to pas laimein
moin.

— Creole folk song

As if a sorcerer struck a flame
to banish night, you were gone.
Only a wisp of plumb rain
sets the dip of moon against
the sky.

I cannot remember the figure of your
face, or the jaunt of your limbs
like an awkward boy running from
the cold.
Yet you singe my heavy dreams.

I will hold you in my mouth
like salt,
a talisman against the odds of
one dusky night throwing all her
stars.

La lumière

Quand la lune est au visage plein,
Mo va posé un poeme
Sur so sein
De sorte que
Quand la lune té parti
To sera capable souffler mes paroles
Et connais que mo té là.

When the moon is full,
I will place a poem
On your bosom
So that
When the moon is gone
You will breathe my words
And know that I was there.

63

Soulangai

FOR MY BROTHERS AND SISTERS

"Memory is everything"
— Osbey

There was a house by the river,
a house that sang with the rising
of soft morning. In the dirt yard,
children would play like June bugs;
slender voices entwined with clucks
from banty hens amid ripening figs,
merlitons, and blackberries. Red
mosquito-hawks posed on clothespins
and spotted butterflies zig-zagged
around hand scrubbed wash. Morning-
glories closed blue over thick slats
of wooden fence on the left side of the house.

There was a house by the river,
a house that sang with the searing afternoon sun.

On the right side, wild roses grew
in the white stone-lined garden near
day-lilies which knew to blossom at
Easter. Often, a young hummingbird
Would linger near the bright hibiscus and
ritually at sundown, small fingers clipped
red, yellow, and white specked four o'clocks
to string ringlets for a handsome baby's hair.
Beneath the healing elephant ears were chunks
of red brick. Evenings, it was expected task
to crush soft brick to powder for cleaning the
grey wood steps at the front of the house.

There was a house by the river,
a house that glistened as the light of dark descended.

Inside at night, an oil lamp on the mantelpiece
bounced wicked shadows on the ochre ceiling;
the flame made quick glances at the dark
pictures of religion and kin. There was reason
to believe that the house was haunted. Uneasy
ghosts weaved in and out of the thin walls at
will. They left their anger on holiday arguments
which hung in the air until past midnight. Pleas,
prayers did no good; words became spectre-knives
to cut the flesh of feeling. But this was the house
that sang, and tears were part of the singing.

There was a house by the river,
a house that moaned under the yoke of the moon.

It was the mother whose voice made
harmony with children's fears, father's
frustrations, the outside world. It was
a voice that swept aside spiteful poverty,
arranged a glory of stars to cover those
cruel storms. It was the mother who broke
the curse of vengeful haunts with her songs,
songs which evoked the souls of ancestors to
foredoom such brute intrusions. And it was the
mother who sang, even to the white stone-lined
grave covered with petals of wild roses thrown
there by the hands of startled children.

There was a house by the river,
a house that shuddered at the footsteps of grief.

It was the father who pitied none;
whose arms never broke under the tillage
of bricks, who knew nothing of finery or
freedom, of gold or grandeur. And it was
the father who bled like a woman until his
body wore thin and white. It was the father
who whistled as he dug holes in the ground,
in the sky, in the wind, to hide what money
was left for another kind of pain. It was
the father who was struck mute because he
saw no use for singing, but who kept
the song in his eyes. And it will be
the children who will carry the secrets
of song to give to memory, to circle the need.

There was a house by the river,
a house that sang with the rising of soft morning.

The Diaspora and the Revolution

FOR LISA C. MOORE

Louisiana

1895.   I.   Apartheid.

Run, run across
to Freedom; all
who can with your
blue eyes or your father's
hair and your gold and your
children, plowmen and poets.

Where is Freedom?
in your soul?
across that Mason-
"Dixie" line? California?
Chicago? New York? Michigan?
Yes? And even in this south?

Change the spelling of your name.
Bid the darker ones go to Brazil,
Mexico, Cuba, anywhere; or bid them
heartbreaking farewell forever.
Beg, bribe them never to reveal
your escape. *Merci Bon Dieu!*
Come by the hundreds, catch that
train, brothers and sisters and
passé, passé, passé on to freedom.
No?
Be black then,
counted with former
slaves: Negroes, African-
Americans, plowmen and poets.

Take up John Brown's sword of
Justice for that long, tortuous
crusade.
We'll come a-inching along,
millions with our schemes
and our plans and God-Help-Us
we shall overcome.

Someday.
Soon.

1995.   II.

Have not those who remained
to die, fight, dealt a mortal
wound to that abomination?
Are we not, then, all free
people?

We hear the last rattling
breath of slavery and we
must bury that beast along
with his colored excuses
for hatred.

Despots have fallen,
walls have come a-tumbling
down and the marrow of man
confirms that none must be
subjugated, beaten, burned,
plundered, razed;
that when the beast is finally
dead, we may salvage the last

of his prey, the ignorant,
the dispossessed, that all must
be vigilant, never again bondage,
apartheid, holocaust; that this
unholy division converge as a
final oneness of all.

Lullaby

Beautiful dreamer:
night after storm;
tall canes creaking
across sugar fields.

Babe in my tired arms
grown half asleep;
soft light of stars
blushing his face.

River is hushed, oh,
winds bound away;
only slow raindrops
melting on trees.

Soundless moon drifting
on indigo sky,
kindling quiet color
and scent of fresh rain.

I do not wake him
from hobby-horse dreams;
but bear him to cradle
and breathe him this song.

Gombo Ya-Ya

FOR ROBERT HAYDEN

New Orleans.
There's no mystery here,
except that contrived for
rapid tourists. Spangled
harlot preachers frame
a tour-de-force, their
gold teeth flash on local
t.v., click over radio waves.
So much to save: wide-eyed
sinners, streetwalkers, rift-
raft, righteous homebodies.

Oh, they let the good times
roll, Zulu and Rex cascade
on silver dust and rhinestones
past stranded houses, dance a
plastic "mawdi-graw;" picayune,
copper cent, almighty dollar's
lean and low.

Brazen racist politicians
would raise the confederacy,
blinking hate and cold cash
to the applause of rebel
necks and hollow heads. Will
this South rise again?
There's a drawl in "y'all,"
and *"cher"* is rarely heard.

I have watched that sullen river
veer and lull, ships like old men,
pace and pause, and move on;
and bleary-eyed death with his
crack smile stakes out streets,
jokes about Indians and half-
black men.

Too much I remember is long
dead, *belles and beaux,* hearth,
home. But antiques and mammy dolls
are still sold in the French Quarter,
there is moss on the trees at Audubon
Park, and the roses, God bless them,
are always in bloom like there is no
tomorrow.

Ghosts

FOR MICHEL FABRE

They raged reason against
hypocrisy, culled dignity
from a fragile freedom,
died for equity, for Art,
for love of humanity.

Dare to reckon?
Dare to name?

Who would embrace them
even now, these *gens de
couleur* of Louisiana?
Lanusse, Warbourg, Dédé,
Rillieux, DeLille, Séjour,
Lafon, for each a thousand
more.

Despite the audacity of
a third acronym, race,
culture, African and European
conjoined as bone, heart,
mind to produce this progeny.

And even as shadow
these gifted Creoles,
their deeds, belie man's
most barbarous error:
the perversion of color
as hoax, as cannon, as
dominion over the oneness
of all souls.

73

Legacy

My father's hands were rough,
swollen from callous labor,
disfigured from cuts and
gashes that scabbed over
years of desperate attempts
at survival.
His slim figure bent under
jobs of hauling, lifting,
digging, under sun that beat him
to his knees, in cold and rain
that sickened him almost to death.
His dignity was battered daily
by bossmen who used him as fool;
he could not chance to answer their
catcalls, curses, foul jokes.

Such a life without hope of change
left him sometimes a cruel ghost.
His humanity raw, he did not know
self-pity, would not tolerate
failure.
He named love in
bright silent acts, his life
as caretaker, father.

If he had dreams of personal glory,
fortune, we never knew them.
We only knew he could grow a tree
from seeds, take an animal from death's
mouth with a secret herb, cure the
stinging wounds of children with
ancient remedies, give them joy
on sleepless cold nights with stories
about "Patcherah," or a magic trick, or
dancing fingershadows of swans on the
walls.

Well, all is done now, laughter, pain. He left
us each other, nothing more.
Nothing more is needed.

En Lafayette

POUR KATHY BALL, CAROLYN DURAL,
ET CONSTANCE MARTEL-MASON

Créole vacherons avec yé
chère femmes dance zydeco
pas de deux, valse, si doux
à El Sid O's. La musique
chante de trois cent l'années,
de moune qui joué, travaillé,
moune qui fait le Créolité avec
yé lavie. Mais plus
que ça, ces moune
parle leur dignité,
la verité de humanité-ça-yé:
Nous sommes Européen, Indian et Africain,
Mais nous sommes aussi Américain.
Ecouté le fier dans nous chansons
en Lafayette et tout z.autre villes
dans la compagne de Bayou:
de l'amour, de la lutte pour être
content, de la foi, espoir, courage.
Ecouté: Créole Inc.-là,
Ecouté: le journal de Créole Culture,
Ecouté: Le Société Preserver de Culture
Créole Français d'Amérique,
Ecouté: La Place Créole.
Ici reste le sang de mon
l'ancestres-yé, c'est moquenne
sang-là; et comme ça,
dans cette zydeco joie de vivre,
malgré tout quichose mal,
nous dance, nous dance, nous dance!

At Lafayette

FOR KATHY BALL, CAROLYN DURAL,
AND CONSTANCE MARTEL-MASON

Creole cowboys with their
lovely women dance zydeco
two step, waltz, so gently
at El Sid O's. The music
sings of three centuries
of people who played, worked,
people who made Creoleness
with their lives. They speak their
dignity, truth of their humanity:
We are European, Indian and African,
but we are also American.
Listen to the pride in our songs
at Lafayette, and all the other
cities of the Bayou Country:
of love, the struggle for happiness,
faith, hope, courage.
Listen to: Creole Inc.,
Listen to: Creole Culture Magazine,
Listen to: The French Creole Preservation
Society of America,
Listen to: The Creole Place.
Here lives the blood of my ancestors,
this is my own blood here.
And in this zydeco joy of life,
despite everything adverse,
we dance, we dance, we dance!

Thibodaux

FOR MARY L. MORTON

THE MASSACRE OF NOVEMBER 22, 1887

Surely there was also the warmth
of *Fur Elisa* from a piano, and
a noble voiced soprano raised
"He Leadeth Me" for next Sunday's
sermon. There must have been
cotton lace in the making by
brown hands unaware of distant
danger, and the first cooing
laugh of a newborn caught by
eyes of surprised parents. Someone
must have baked a sweet potato pie
for aunt and uncle, married fifty
years; and someone must have blenched
at the roar of whispered hate, those
sins of indifference.

When the first shots were fired, as
the striking cane workers, the Creoles
who led them were hacked with machetes,
as death lay on the road, bloated the
river, rustled the frost on the trees,
surely someone wept like raging rain.
Tales of panic, tales of fear from
hiding the strikers, tales of lynchings
and worst stunted this town. The Knights
of Labor lost its cause, its core. Those
who did not die went back to the fields
for seven dollars a month; any wounded
Creoles fled forever. Planters' mansions
huddled, crumbled, most, like the Confederacy,
would struggle and fall.

Thibodaux sits small, perhaps a little lonely
in its silvan landscape. There are no Creoles
of color here, but there are people like you,
Mary Morton, who by their wisdom, bravely
harbor true southern kindness; and those of us
who fear the present past may breathe free and
for a while, forgive.

GLOSSARY

bamboula social and religious slave dance.

Beaumont, Creole writer of poems and songs in
Joseph (1820-1872) early 19th century New Orleans.
"Toucoutou" is the only extant song
of hundreds which he wrote.

banquette sidewalk

calas Creole rice cake originated by
African-American women who
worked as food peddlers in old
New Orleans.

calinda slave dance — a social square dance
performed in Congo Square, New
Orleans.

chèr Creole language term of endearment.

Coincoin African name for Marie Thérèse
Metoyer, founder of the Metoyer clan
in Natchitoches, Louisiana.

Congo Square Place Congo, a public square in 18th
and 19th century New Orleans where
slaves were allowed to gather for
recreation.

cordon bleu literally, "blue ribbon" — the original
name of the social club founded in
the mid-1700's by aristocratic free
women of color to protect their
daughters from slavery. These
women developed a system known as
"plaçage" wherein European men

81

were contracted to provide financial security for the women and their resulting offspring for life, in exchange for a romantic relationship with the woman. This was a romantic and business arrangement. La Société du Cordon Bleu presented the first of their balls or debutante parties in the 18th century in New Orleans. Later, these balls became known as quadroon balls. They were imitated by white businessmen who hired prostitutes of all races to preside over public dances designed to profit from the fame of the original. These latter were held until the mid-1930's.

Creole

a Louisiana native of mixed heritage usually including African, French, Spanish and Native American.

Dédé

Edmond Dédé (1829-1901), composer, violinist. This famed musician was conductor of orchestras in Bordeaux, France for twenty-five years. He wrote hundreds of selections of classical music including an unfinished opera started just before his death.

Delille

Henriette Delille (1813-1862), free woman of color who, along with Josephine Charles and Juliette Gaudin, founded Les Soeurs de la Sainte Famille, The Sisters of the Holy Family in 1843. This Catholic order of nuns still thrives in New Orleans.

Ézilie

Female goddess of love and protector of women and children — from the Haitian Voodoo pantheon.

fais-do-do	an Acadian dance.
filé	ground sassafras used in seasoning Creole gumbo. A Native American herb.
gens de couleur libres	free people of color — a designation given to Creoles in 18th and 19th century Louisiana.
gombo ya-ya	Creole language term for "gossip."
joli blon	Acadian/Creole term — can be compared to "negresse," both meaning "sweetheart."
Legba	Male deity of the Haitian Voodoo pantheon found in rara and petro groups. Guardian of the crossroads.
Lanusse	Armand Lanusse (1812 -1867), editor of *Les Cenelles,* the first published African- American anthology in 1845. He was poet, teacher, and civil-rights advocate.
McDonogh	John McDonogh (1779-1850), a multi-millionaire Scottish philanthropist who trained and freed his slaves in Louisiana. He left part of his fortune to establish free schools for the poor in his native Baltimore and New Orleans. He left his son, Francis, child of Carmelite Pena, $100,000 in his will.
merliton	a vegetable found in Louisiana, a form of squash.
Natchez	A tribe of Native American people who were one of several groups found in the Louisiana Territory.

passé or passé blanc	Creole term meaning to pretend to be Caucasian, to live as Caucasian.
Père Antoine	Antonio de Sedella, a Capuchine priest who was sent from Spain to establish the Inquisition in New Orleans. He later became curé of the St. Louis Cathedral until his death in 1829. A very liberal-minded and kindly man, he is said to have "married" according to church rites many of the quadroon women and their European men. (The marriages were recorded in the side books of the cathedral.) "Père Antoine Cheri," as he was called by the *gens de couleur libres,* was a trusted friend of these Creoles.
picayune	Spanish-American half-real piece used in old Louisiana, probably equivalent to British half-penny.
praline	A Creole candy made of pecans cooked in brown sugar. Sold by slaves and free women of color in Louisiana.
quarteronne	French term for quadroon or free woman of color. Said to be the most beautiful women in the world, often of French and Senegalese extraction. They were romanticized as "les sirenes" and negatively stereotyped as "tragic mulatto," "yella gal," and vile seductress.
St. Expédit	Catholic/Voodoo saint said to bring quick luck.
Séjour	Victor Sejour (1819-1867?), poet and playwright. He spent most of his life in France to escape the racism of

Louisiana. There he, like many of his contemporaries, achieved international fame and success. Twenty or more of his plays were performed in many theaters in Paris.

Sun God   High god of the Natchez people.

tignon   A madras head scarf —18th century Louisiana. An ordinance of Governor Miro's in 1788, forbade the free women of color to wear "silks, jewels or plumes." The European women complained that their men gave all their time and attention to these Creoles. The purpose of this ordinance was to render them less beautiful. Of course, it did not serve to hide their beauty, but enhanced it.

Warbourg   Eugene Warbourg. Creole sculptor who studied in Paris and became world known for his work in the 19th century. He did commissions for the St. Louis Cathedral and for other prominent historic buildings.

zydeco   Rural Creole dance music.